a clone of my heart! In one story it's like, 'Yes!
I can jump from the highest mountain without
am invincible!' The next story's like, 'Yes! That's
no energy to scale the mountain, but who
t to get out of bed.' There are many con-
his book helps me feel normal also nice to
el the ups and downs like I was reading this
normal after all!"

Heat

14

lonely because you get used to
you think you're pretty great or pr
g board, a measuring stick, a b

Brad Chan

Steve Smith

tronaut and veteran of two space flights,
dred Earth orbits and three space walks

vas inspired by the kindness and gener-
s reporting on things they had done. I am
they have for the world. It is also evident
ay's teens can—and will—change the

Ronald Glosser

ce chairman of the board, Guideposts

ke to be a teenager—there is such a
d of bad. *Taste Berries for Teens* h
o together, and in keeping with t
bad tolerable. Read this remarka
to use the stage of adolescence
on in our young people."

Janice Will

AmeriCorps–21st Century Sch

favorite ones you own, and th
hink deeply about what you
to become, and to decide
d about other teens and le
es relevant to teens living
tacular challenges. An c

Lauren

Building C